THE HOLY MERRIMENT

THE
HOLY
MERRIMENT

ARNOLD KENSETH

Chapel Hill

The University of North Carolina Press

CONTEMPORARY POETRY SERIES

Library of Congress Catalog Card Number 63-21078

PRINTED BY THE SEEMAN PRINTERY, DURHAM, N. C.

Manufactured in the United States of America

FOR MY WIFE
AND WISEST CRITIC
BETTY

CONTENTS

SERMON TO MYSELF

A
CYCLE
OF PRAISE

A CYCLE OF PRAISE

The roads of our village amble
Through views of four seasons.
The eye loves and follows
The ritual year through occasions
That dazzle all seeing, humble
All knowing. Changes are heard:
Spring drums in the little hollows,
The to-and-fro borne bird
Of summer chirrs, the pageant
Autumn trumpets on the hills.
All sceneries lie urgent
On the heart. All are a praise
To Him whose laughter wills
Our glory-be of days.

Especially now do we feel
His sounding joy and His dare:
When sun-dials point winter
And daylights grow fainter;
When Advent hallows our streets
In a snowfall of prayers.
From windows our fire-trees
Wink azure devotions,
Because His birth bells peal
Alarums of love at our gates,
And we wake with His innocence
In us. The year ends here,
But we begin, in the air's dance
Of bright adorations.

3

AN ADORATION

In this snowfall season the birth
Of God's furious and tender Son
Gives us our holy days by fire. Earth
Cradles once more the hope that Eve
And her winter children will receive
The sunlit garden; because fear
Has no room in our Saviour's castle.

All love shepherds us. The pageant kings
Weep for us. In argent rings
Heaven's wild gabriels wrestle
For our very souls. What stables here
Is time for us to give our sin
The shape of kneeling, to perch seven
Times seventy singing robins

Of forgiveness on our tongues,
Blessing our enemies, that the bones
Which we have broken may rejoice.
No one is lost, not one, who yields
Himself to Christmas. The red ribbons
Of his grief adorn us. The voice
Of his mercy is heard in our fields.

SNOW STORM

Outside the night is winter.
Snow goes dying down the road.
Cold rocks the window's crevice
Where the wind has slowed.

The storm goes murmuring out
To howl the unmarched town,
The white flakes follow the dark
Upward and down.

I see my neighbors' houses
Lying like boxes and lost
In the lightless weather of sleep
Under roofs of frost.

The yards are drifted in,
The shapes are blurred and far,
More mysteries than homes
Where humans are.

And hissing against the pane
The blizzard pauses for breath,
And troubles me there in the dark
By its talk of death,

Or maybe of faith, whichever
Loneliness chooses
To counter the muffled blow
The storm looses.

BROWN CREEPER

I know, I know how it will be
Whether the bird with brown wings
Flies heavenward or no. He returns
To what the tree is—roughed with winter,
Cold as any man's foodless table.

Both are necessary: flight and fall.
What is indescribable is why?

It starts with morning.
The brown bird comes pleased.
The wind-beat is his. His hooked bill
Slender for labor, like a mind,
Probes out the lilac's poverty,
Its summer deadness here.

Say, then,
The election of saints is so:
To joy to leave the air and go
To a cold tree, to work
Over a plain thing . . . with wings.

LUCIFER

The grackle comes.
Winter's black weather
Walks beside him hard
Who is the spring's
Dark brooding lord.

An arrogance,
He sits aloft, disdains
The tipping winds, shrugs
Off the shaking cold
Of April rains.

His yellow eye
Marks how the tight buds tire
Holding soft summer in:
He waits the thaw,
The flower, the fire.

His flight to earth
Is falling dark. Like one
Who also fell,
His charcoal wings
Still shoulder sun.

A COLLECT FOR COMPASSION

There in the rudest tree
Where winter grips and rocks
The black indefinite cold,
Comes the small chickadee,

And like my soul, pipes
Anxious prayer, implores
An opening of doors,
Some crust and surety.

My hand, give him his bread!

May whirlwind God pause
From His storms and come
To me with Cup and Crumb.

THIS BLUE DAY COMES FAIR

This blue day comes fair
By sun rising from under.
O wanderer in us here,
Do you see fire burning
Out ache, anger, plunder?

From south today
Breath sallies forth,
Blows in warm gusts
God's dare, man's despair,
Field, road, hill over.

O how on kite days
No man cries pity,
But walks firm, thinks sure,
When earth lifts it shoulder
And the great sun stirs.

AFTERNOON STROLL

Belled and querulous with song
Bluebirds hang upon the wire
Flute-light merry and higher
Than plod, plan, or man's brash tongue.

All around them rush and power:
Jay's yah-yah, red truck's churn, our
Foot-ring human hard below.
But undisturbed the bluebird row

As if air's white summer paused
In their song's center, their talk
Of some deeper inner blue,
Like the first sky on man's first walk.

THUNDERSTORM

This evening could be outer darkness. Clouds
Prophecy; and one gigantic nimbus
Reaches swords and fire enough to tame us
Who thought we had a safety zone in crowds.

Moving like last judgment on the woods,
The black wind falls on us, and covers all
We felt were certain and familiar goods,
And shakes the roof and blows against the stall;

And powers increasingly against the town
A rain of wet apocalyptic terror
To flood away our arks of human error;
And we are watered in who watered down.

But what was last was only latest judgment;
The house withstood, and so had fence and barn.
The stars came out, as if the storm's intent
Was to forgive or, at the worst, to warn.

JUNE GALES

The yellow wing that summer stretches far
Snaps at the wind's edge, the mind's edge,
The soft month blows itself away.

Yesterday's swans have drifted off,
The evening robin sings in other gardens,
The white lilies float away downstream.
The striking hour is gone, the bells
Corrode, the steeple falls, white turns to grey,
Over trellises the thorn runs wild.

The June gales riped us without mercy;
A marching to old drums bruised us,
There was a claw in men's minds.
We who loved summer sickened there,
 For the swimming softness, night's mothering,
Did not stay.

Air turned grey and cold. We aged
Under its columns. The morning sky held
The sun no longer, no longer the rainbow.
Nothing but the crabbed, the cribbed,
The roads dust-ridden, the choked acres.

The weather's accident confounds us.
Our days stand in middle darkness.
Always the whirlwind is in us,
The true destruction that unpeoples
Our little natural cities of desires,
Strips off old ornament and ease, centers
The self's dark dread.

O isolating storm,
No season knows you, no, nor dares
Over earth plunge with a cleansing wind
Into such joyous dark, such violent birth.
Elsewhere the battle is phantom, futile;
Among these terrors, precisely here,
Falls downward the morning star.

ELEGY

It was there I went
In the hot summer
To the dried field
Behind spruces, intent

On the priest cry
Of the mourning doves.
O the amen, the amen,
Low and sad in that field

Dried and withered
Like the world,
Where the doves shook joy
From the dust in the hollows.

But never a dove was seen.
Only the amen's fall
And its fade-away
Far among trees.

POEM IN AUTUMN

The sky is not the same: not brighter but
Closer, its breath running as it does
Behind people's faces, its press on grass.
Its spinning out in moving golden bundles
Everywhere persists in me like touch.

Suspicions of winter perplex us only.
The merchant birds that once came north singing,
Crying turn south. Twice we have heard them
On the night air, their small and treble pipes
Scattering sounds over the autumn cities.

The silence that follows expands in us.

Our daylight walks assure us, and we fear
Only the human weather: the heavy tread,
Steel on the land, and overhead, death
Trailing like smoke across the wounded air.

THE TREE AS A SHIP

The tree in a sea of air
Is an old tree in an old sea,
Is a ship creaking under the winds
Or drying in sun and tasting green.
It is a great mast shaking in the small breath
Of summer, its leaves waking
And rising and falling and making
Sail. Or it is the ship's body,
Its trunk a dark hulk
And its branches a buoyancy
On the air's ocean. Old tree,
Over so many years you have journeyed:
Catching the breeze in your nets,
In your bow-sprit and spanners;
Holding the great grave green air
Of summer, tossing it back and forth
In the easy gales; or bending
To the black storm's churn and chase
How many thousand days?
And each autumn you become galleon,
Riding the cool days browsy and ready,
Turning magnificently your power to all violence,
Until it is you who are master,
In control, wealthy and brimming.
In winter port you strip down,
And the masts spring up black and higher,
The white ocean sprays you with snow,
And your vast age and bulk and excitement
                    Wait.

BIRDS AT THE FEEDING STATION

In the brown branches the forsythia
Fountains, arching and falling and trailing
All winter; the air is wings and sailing
And landing and eating. What is rosier
Than the red poll's blurred breast, or more golden
In perches of snow than grosbeaks' swooped
Yellows, or bluer than cocked jays who fold in
Their feathers the sky combed and caped?
Or what is more rainbow?
      Such covenant
Is here as Noah won. Green waters' weight
Around his world, he saw the promises
In colors drenching down from heaven's gate,
And felt man's hope, awash and innocent,
Sung where the hosts anoint. Then, clamorous,
His bridled birds broke free, arose in rings
Spontaneous, proposing love for Love.

And still they circle in our snowy grove
Azure and pied, incarnadine and blaze,
Rocking the hemlocks white with carollings,
Making our windows tapestries of praise.

BY MAN
CAME DEATH'S
NATIVITY

BY MAN CAME DEATH'S NATIVITY

The heavy habit of death that in man lies
Is not the bone box where he stores his flesh;
Nor yet the cave-in of his breath whose airs rush
Lost from his lungs' room and his windless eyes,
His blood ox-bowed and finally in his veins
All stilled; nor folded in his porcelain hands,
Nor imaged in the mannikin remains
Dress-suited, rouged beside the flower stands.

Death is too lively; death companions sin.
When the sun burst in man's chest, after God
Birthed heaven and the apple mountained in
The tree: by man came death's nativity.
And man, unfathered by his lightning, fled ...
And split himself asunder to be free.

A WALK IN THE EVENING

In the very green of the evening
When day sprints to hush and hurry is slow,
And airs without murder are havening
The just and the jilted, the yes and the no;
When always and good are like browse and bell
Under wires where swallow-wings converse
Of ever forever, while red barns dwell
Easy, and crickets of kindness rehearse:

Everyman as yet by death unsummoned
(The kilroyed, aliced, pauled, or simple-simoned)
Saunters in shirt sleeves down his thousand walks
To find a garden clad in white and fire,
Before the fruit comes out, before desire,
Before the whispering serpent wakes and talks.

MEDITATION IN AUTUMN

High with red leaves and sounds sharp sweeping
Overhead like squalls of quick brown birds,
Autumn, that desperate yellowing time,
Blows, burns me with an unsettling grace.

Roads that were summer wear a scarlet terror.
Dark scowl of sky on afternoon descends
On man in solitary, pairs, or crowds,
Who toward the heavens' wilderness lifts human eyes.

This falling-rising, branches, gold, fire,—Whose?
And for what flight do we who gather here,
Like flocks of frightened geese, raise loudly
Clumsy wings against the grey winds' plough?

Emptying fearfully our thin last strength
Into what calm seasons do we come at length?

TRAIN RIDE

The train we ride scouts curves of human houses,
Observer's voyage on a double track:
The sailor sags, the high-school boy carouses;
Anxiety is here, and love, and lack.

Outside, the hollyhock people bob from gardens,
Waving us gladly on from private plots;
We see ourselves, but pity in us hardens:
We smoke the cigarette of private thoughts.

Down through the woods of wishing and of maple,
We rush to meet green, scarlet, fact and dream;
The journey's end is judgment and is papal:
No easy firesides with eggs and cream.

Close pastures blur; the tipped sky races.
And each observer searches his own glass
For one clear meadow in the rush of places,
One lofty open pause within the mass.

OFFICE BOY

I live too close in narrow rooms,
My breath partaking the small air and myself
There at the desk proudly, safe and sure,
Stroking the soft body of the calendar.

This is the small man's destiny, this ease;
This saying Yes to certain smiling men.
At five the window-stick, five-one the lock,
Homeward on leash to comfort by the clock.

In the round air the proud sun;
And over roofs and houses space bends
Day, and after it the night sends
Darkness. Is it so with everyone?

Ah, bitter to be haltered here,
Having nuzzled sun, to crop their favor;
When I despise their soft silk minds
And in my heart the towering world turns over.

B-52's

Against summer, the leaf-lovely wide and lively trees,
The bird songs wild and tanager, the saint's walk,
And the sermon where the brown sparrows toss and talk;
Against the fields' burn of hay and mowers, the degrees
Of meadow upon meadow rising and running far and away;
Against all this, against lovers and the heart's day,
Against daybreak and daylight and holy delight,

They have instrumented death, under and overhead.

I am filtered through by the ooze.
I smell their blind eyes
Touch the child sleeping who does not know.
Like blue flies
They hover against summer.
They lean over and touch the rose dead.

HOW THEY CAME FROM THE BLUE SNOWS

How they came from the blue snows year after year
Into the stranger's arbor, under the rain;
Hearing the sandhill cranes at night, marching again
To the next continent with the great spear
Of starlight flying before them as they go
Into the africas, americas, exploring
Tomorrow and the place, sun pouring
Laughter, and an oracle always on the winds.

Now do we track the tiger in the mind.
Now do the swift deer leap the nerve and bone;
It snows in the heart. We penetrate
A dry and sunless continent of stone;
And the flight of birds from the summer hollow
We do not understand, we do not follow.

DAYLIGHT LEANING

At the dusk there is flower
That is not flower but shadow,
At the dusk climbs the half-light.
Emerges from day like a leopard
The night alone and everywhere
Hunting, everywhere turning
With death and returning with terror.
This at the dusk, this in the night
Come down after the dusk
Climbing from day softly.

O in the night remember the day,
Calmly upon a river bank waiting:
A traveler, dreamer, cloak wide
With the sun as he strides into morning.
Mountains are light on his fingers,
Sunlight is bronze on his palms;
The earth is his drum, and he shouts!
And he dreams: O delicate swing
Of the architect mind after God
Praising thee, O Jerusalem.

In the night do not wait insidiously.
It is not for this: neither evil
Nor dying; not for body, the sick love,
Sensation, nor the opium sway
Of the mind toward a grievance.
It is the self in the animal
Singing after the self in the cloud;
And the cloud gone now, dissolving,
The dusk climbing from day,
The night come down, and daylight
Leaning from the leopard's eyes.

CHANTICLEER

The green of the rooster pauses among the hens.
Hear the luck-luck talk of the plump reds running
For the feed. Come, biddie, biddie, biddie. Sunning,
The yellow cat is a lioness, and dozes. Brown tens
Of sparrows beak in the barn eaves, then dry leaf
Down and settle in the grain spill. A blue thief
Yah-yahs from the sky for corn. The air protests,
Bothers for a moment. Then the morning rests.

It is all fair and lazy, so easy, so easy.
I have it in my eyes and I hear it as if my skin
Were in the cat's elegance, in the browsy
Stretch of her claws. Somewhere I found it in
An idling, in a spell-bound me, in an image.
True, the green cock is not Peter's bird. No rage
Is in him. He is a bronze king among the nervous
Sparrows, and he walks among his matrons in peace.

JACOB

All, everywhere, and now, and high and low,
The moonlight meadows, shadows, blows its candles
In the corn, strikes midnight barns, and fondles
Walls, elms, and every sleeping thing below.

Mists pad and curl and cool. Effortless air
Ladders with lanterned angels up and down.
I stand like Jacob heavened in, aware
Of warless music sung above the town.

If it were only so! The awakened bell
Of cattle in the night, the shining span
Of almost wings on grass, the world's All's Well
An always sent to somewhere private man,

Who in a deeper night wrestles black Why,
Finds blessing in the wound, the limping thigh.

NOTE FOR A MARRIAGE VOW

I hear you in accents not spoken by men.
O many silent tongues speak through you,
And I believe it is good to love this way.

There are many things said, the speech of many men
And their words on paper urging us: act! be ready!
And many men die by words, run over by words

And rolling in dust on highways for listening well
But not wisely. Some have been saved
To speak more words, to write epitaphs.

I have awaited the speech of many other women:
Sometimes at night falling on pavements
The clear trickling laugh, the invitation;

Sometimes the speech like stone, heavily,
Inquiring, wondering. The idea gone,
Only the form, the broken word remaining.

I have heard and have not heard.
There is pain in the world, there is evil;
There is pain and there is too much talking.

Your speech has pain in it,
But your silence has in it another pain
Which comes from anywhere but here and now.

This is a joy that has no home.
It meets me in lonely places. It is like
Nothing on earth. It has no name.

It speaks, and my hands shout for binding you to me
Forever. It does not speak, and I stand
Hearing giants walk the corners of my heart.

PLANE SONG

Gunners are silent near the sun.
The stricken airman falls undone
At heaven's gate and falls in fire,
A crippled sparrow to the briar.

Evil on wings, on wings descends,
To death descends, its evil ends;
And ends machine and man who kill.
Gunners beneath the sun are still.

CHRISTMAS 1941

In plain December, crisp gift,
God's child bows us here,
Breaks us by joy's soft blows,
Kneels us, strips us,
Pares pride, gives ache,
And doth with chiming words
Raise up the people, level grief,
Grip hard, hurl wide his bold,
His ringing rage across the world.

METAPHOR IN OCTOBER

At what hour a man finds his dying
Depends on timing and symbol:
The use of the senses by grace,
The slowing of worlds to the amble
Of love that can hold the flying
And distorted discs in place,
In cinemas of air and rush
Can photograph the burning bush.

I speak against decoration.
Thus, nature is insufficient
In itself to rage or to send
Color by birds, the magnificent
Errands of clouds, the stare
Of sun; except metaphor
Captures for us nature's end—
Our need for celebration.

So in autumn I see man's death:
How it lies around us in fire;
How it wedges, teases the breath
To utter its exhausted dare;
And watches our footstep advance
Through the ritual smoke, the red dance,
Until the messages are lost,
And mountains fall on us.

THE HANDS OF GOD

The hour is late, the household clocks bell deep.
I hear from room to room the shell-song breath
My three small children, eye-lash long in sleep,
Sigh like the very mourning doves of faith.

And think, as prowling midnight closes in,
How weak they lie, how open to attack
From thief, the bludgeon, bomb, the shipwreck
Dream, the mountains falling, and black Herod's sin;

And fear the winter and the winter cough,
And pray that all men's houses will stand fast,
That innocence will receive love enough,
That the ceremonies of mercy will last.

Then it is, God, I can see your hands,
The gnarled enormous hands that uphold heaven,
Squaring a pillow, pulling up a cover,
Breathing your breath until their breath comes even;

As in the long, long night that never ends,
You brood and father till the rising sun;
And fondly name by name, over and over,
Your sleep-rocked weary children one by one.

PRAY FOR US NOW

In the hospitals the sick are lost
On the mountains of pain. Go who will
With them, they are alone in their forest:
Their dense dreams, sedative and animal;
Their bodies briared and their breath at bay,
Shredding out murmurs, crying out wounds
To the night watch; while our hands of pity
Leaf the dead branches of their feverish hands.

The feeble rivers of their blood are still,
Their gray old age of agonies is done,
Healed by good death who keeps his ritual
With everyman; as in the medicined air
Our griefs huddle with faith, and one by one
Kneel out the brooding majesties of prayer.

NOTE UPON A MANNER OF LIVING

Earth-bound and dragged by body to the feast,
The Smiths enjoy snug comfort at the table,
Imbibe their drinks, attend the current fable
At the Orpheum. Happy is the beast
When the blood purrs, happy when belly heat
Mounts from the body's furnace to the chin;
When sex, sly and with padded house-cat feet,
Walks on the maiden membranes of the skin.

And now arouse the napping bones and drive
Home to the old adventure of the bed,
To stroke the animal to sleep, to wed
Forgetfulness again, and so survive.
For midnight at the corner is alive
And sky is falling inward overhead.

SATAN

Stern, stern, under
Old ocean, wind you now!
Devil you are: plotting,
Marking with bone
Circle around us.
Net-drawn, soul-drawn, how
You grapple us under,
Making moan, moan.

O we have sea-edged
Heard the god's sky-cry,
As the breath shocked,
Shook in the morning air.
Aye, we were for climbing
Within us. Ho! high
To the windy places
Spiralled our stair.

But ever the dark claw
Wheedles us. Cleft
We are, captured, devil!
Doomed, doubly undone!
You split the stairway,
Terror, terror! Deft,
Deft, you wield us, drive us,
Pitch us from the sun.

AUTUMN PENTECOST

The pouring love is God's
And everywhere is pentecost.
Trees once green are swirls,
Streets are in leaf-drift lost.
Children's voices toss the flames,
The bright balls of laughter,
Into delighted air.
Their quick small steps ring loud
Under the sky's great hill.
A man must turn now. Fall
Is brimming over him
More than the human fires.
Winds are racing inward,
Oak and maples bending;
Earth's grass presses him breath
And bone. The time is full
Of endlessness trying
To burn a man down
To a clear flash, a shining.

WINTER RECOLLECTION

Winter's trees are windowed
And the light-filled dark bends
Through them. I go and you, brother,
Homeward as the twilight ends.

Cold sky leans against us.
Winter's short breath breaks in spaces
In the lung's arch. Bone braces.
We step across the rutted land.

How the night-wind prods us along
Through hard air, drives us together,
Good comrade, you and I, who know so well
The contest in the human weather.

Ah, but the night's rise everywhere over us
Unburdens now its thousand bright pure stars:
Eternal on their shining hills they rest;
We rest upon our shining wars.

AS IF WITH ANGELS

As if with angels, God isaiahs me.
I am charred, I am sick; but He bears fire,
Rekindles, heals. As Blake saw in a tree
Branches of wings, painted a hidden choir;

So I write down the versions of my joy,
Because these holy ones guest in my heart,
Wander my blood, make my glad bones employ
Themselves deft and daily in the earnest art

Of adoration. For Blake knew well why
We are here. He saw in all things and flesh
The altar lifted up, the scarlet flash
That tongs God's coal of mercy to the tongue.

So I am, first, my death. After I die,
Then I am burned and birthed. All life amazes,
And I become God's man, His morning bell rung
Back and forth in ever-after praises.

MARRIAGE SONG

Now in the savory May, my love, rest easy,
Rest easy here in my arms like a lady
Comforting her lord who is most unlordly,
Home from the small unenchanted wars, hazy
In honors, griefed in between the worldly
And unworldly, in your devotion steady.
I desire only to love you. Be easy,
Be easy under my hands like a dove,
A mourning dove in the bluewater morning
Somewhere turning her breast all lazy
In rose-dust and sun. I will enter
Your daylight. Lie easy. Lie lovely.
The maned unicorn trembles near the grove
Of honey, as down the undulant valleys
And over, ten soundless ponies canter
On pink hooves tentative and lively,
And allelulias rung on little bells
Of breath ring changes on the rituals
With joy, till phoenixed on a hill of fires
The dazzled flesh enjoys and then adores.

DÜRER'S NATIVITY

Dürer in woodcuts blacked-lined in
Two worlds and almost made them one:
Blazed heaven down on Bethlehem,
Turreted mad Jerusalem
Up into clouds, and hung God's graces
In doves above his peasants' faces.
He read the pouted lips of sin
Even in those who praised the Son.

So he drew Mary plain and round
As any mother-Mary found;
Cut barn beams, straw, in blocks of wood,
Doffed Dick the shepherd's steepled hat
In foolish love. The horned ox stood
Watching God's poverty asleep.
God's wisdom, then, is simply that
The lowly may accept the deep.

Albrecht, this meek festivity
Under the stable's broken roof,
Where tiered-winged angels kneel in love
And dimpled cherubs choir in rings,
Claims us. We cannot stand aloof.
We pray for the descending dove,
The grace of the enfolding wings
On this and all nativity.

YOUR OLD MEN SHALL DREAM DREAMS

The lights in a room are never light
Enough for all. True, a lamp gives importance
To a table, twists an amber dance
About a father reading, the weight

Of his book or the news drowsing him. He is
A dark man within. He does not say
Nor does he know how much of him is day.
His eyes close, and he nods in the phrases

Of sleep. His gray breath sighs under
The green glass chandelier, while his house
Rests dreadful and dour like thunder
Waiting to be heard. A yellow blur, diffuse

Upon the white tablecloth, flattens
His shadow, his sadness. Yet everywhere
Large wonder stirs his dreams, and heightens
In him, and exclaims another air.

His bones hold hide-and-seek, straw fields
At noon and mulberry blouses over
Soft-sung breasts, the azure shiver
Across ponds quickly when the wind unfolds.

He memorizes and loves in memories
What could not stay. He will awake in
Lamp-light and half-dark, muddled as sin,
Still flesh and cough, hunched over knees.

If he is my father or yours, I pray him
A fire dream, such scenery as when
The Holy Ghost, the Child, the cherubim
Captured the dark; and all the old men,

Rising from their death, felt in their glee
God's mercy-making hands, and sang, and heard
The great brass oxen bells, and saw God's burning bird
Die without fear in His nativity.

THE MAGICIAN
(For Ingmar Bergman)

The magician has the stigmata and the wood-cut face.
His sleight-of-hand loves and his eyes are sad.
Is he as tall as night? See, his illusion is his grace:
How he holds the dying man and our dying as if he had
All sorrow in his arms, as if he were his own mother
Cradling Jesus come down from the cross. In his act
His wife becomes a young boy, one to arrange the bother
Of boxes, the stage properties, each artifact
To make invisible (and here the reader must try
To understand) the visible fiction, the observer's lie.

At the trial (by wizardry) he unlooses the tongue of Eve
(A shrewish woman) who tells on Adam (a man who cheats);
And the judges shudder while he binds the two fists of a giant
In mid-air (without thongs). Still, they do not believe.
Their truth, frocked-coated, spectacled, and self-reliant,
Friezes within the room of huge mahoganies. The high seats
Whisper and the jury nods. And so he almost performs
The trick of Lazarus, the hidden figure everyman must know
A summoning by Easter drums to presto-chango!
But the mirrors waken and the place walks with alarms.

Right from the play's beginning the light fell strangely:
The carriage rode through bell-bewitching woods;
The old woman counted money and mumbled stingily;
The manager, fat as fear, saw death arching in the hoods
Of trees; while the young boy, mascaraed and white,
Listened like a bird. The silences of fright
Cried everywhere; and the magician (the mystery)
Entered the pain (for he himself was pain) and went to see
Why the air stopped breathing and the day went dumb.
What of the wickedness in the wood? What of the dead?
Who peoples in the sobbing and the prayers? Whose head
Lies there? What perishes to make the flesh go numb?

In the laundry room the serving girl undoes her blouse
And the coach boy undresses his dreams. She is sun
And he is snow in the linen, and they melt into one
In a washday of sin. Elsewhere in the house
The magician goes to his room, takes off the magic clothes,
Lets fall his mask, becomes as one of us, a man of prose,
A bread and butter man all hungry and unbuttoned down.
See, on the floor, the mask is Jesus' face! Why does a plain
Man with a thin belly, with heron's legs, with a whimper for eyes,
And with a flaxen wife to keep him warm, take this disguise?
Put on God's suffering, wear in his cheeks, his lip-line, the slain
Black look of heaven? All naked, he remains unknown.

At the play's end when the bluebottle policemen swarm
In the hallways; he stands in shreds, the desolate one,
Scarecrow before his betters and accusers. Then clarion
And azure comes the royal word, and he is summoned to perform
Where kings will watch and princes gather to his rising.
Now on his ordinary face (without the mask) deepen
The agonies the mask has worn. Must he convert misshapen
Hearts to pumpkins, dance rainbow mice, make miracle surprising?
Or will the princes know his wand works peace? And if the king
Has faith enough, will waters run again and green leaves catch
The dragonflies of sun? Will speech caress and love bring
Mercy to the crossroads? Will larks arise from the ditch?

Outside the street is sunless. The palace carriage waits.
The coach boy gathers the reins. Beside him his primrose jade
Feathers her skirts, while four pale horses changing gaits
Impatiently, stomp cold and thud the cobblestones aloud.

POETRY READING
(A Criticism on the Poet with the Universal Theme)

He wrote of birds, not bobolinks or robins,
But vague generations of flying: their flight
Going round him like green and pleasant seasons,
Like boys and girls spinning prettily their tops
But with no string attached either to top or hand.
Flowers, too, were general: some mythical blossoms
Falling on New England, powdered with space and time,
Petalled rose, delicately rooted in air's nothing,
As though fragrance were enough to solve man's pain.

True, there were crocuses, daffodils to kiss
Winter into spring; and the universal trees
Waved on spring's banners into summer's rains;
Then, the green leaf tired on the summer bough
And fell bleakly into autumn's red old age;
The cycle closed nicely in winter's drear and blow;
Comfortable eternity piled up on us like snowdrifts.

What was image, picture was moral and uplifting;
Bird, flower, tree, season, time past, time infinite
Were winds leased out for pleasure, for passage
Out of day's hard human trick of sourbread, salt.
He had us legging off on wings, on shining weather,
Skipping the rotted human moment, dodging the bent men
Crowded on our porches. He played cloud games rather.

Listening to his flirt with Truth, I thought of Hopkins
Who taught God's dangerous distances wedged wild
In man's sick unslumbering heart. Of Rilke's angel,
Violent fact, always a hand's length from breath's small beat.
Mostly, I saw One slogging with both feet hard to earth,
Pointing with carpenter's fingers at the great God
On Martha's doorstep, in yeast coin rising wheat and men.

His birds were sparrows briefly winged and down;
His flowers: small mustard seed spawning prisons, whips, hearts;
His tree: one ugly wooden crossbar shaped for nails;
Its roots in lepers, blindmen, Lazarus; its branches,
Heaven's hands and feet stretched, halted human size;
No leaves but blood, sword, bread, and murderous Saul.

I saw a seasonless, single, concentrated Man
Binding Jehovah under a dove's gray common wings.

SERMON
TO
MYSELF

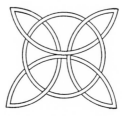

SERMON TO MYSELF

By day I speak the hydra Word of God
That spoken splits in triple-headed flames
To burn the blockhead pews of honest names:
Doctor Judas, Mrs. Good, and Deacon Nod.
They sit, souls folded, as I dare my dare
To set upon their flesh the Three-Faced Beast
Who cuffs straight-backed content to crouched despair,
And strips Man's costumed great to naked least.

At night I trembling lie, dark-wooded in,
While Christ the Child prowls in my brambled heart,
The Dove of Grace harries my hidden sin,
And Six-winged God causes my flesh to start:
For I am Sunday Judas churched in fraud,
Myself am Mrs. Good and Deacon Nod.

NATIVITY

After the conversation
With angels, the winter run
With fear through dreadful wood
To hang a lantern for God's Son:
Were shepherds ever-after good?
Was all work adoration?

Did the lolling black ox tongue
Into the donkey's elder ear:
Behold our Lamb whose mercies take
Away all bridle, blows, and ache!
Were such soft praises sung?
Did any listening human hear?

Mary, being mother, pondered
How Love led the kneeling,
Praised the small sheep crying;
Wept a little, and wondered,
Lonely, as wings were wheeling,
Why Birth knew so much of Dying.

And the Child,
Anointed for sorrow,
Fell asleep in
The Grace of God's Hands.

CHRISTMAS EVE SNOWFALL

Now snow upon our village lays
Its slow but always sudden white
That gives us warmth by falling cold,
Gives glory to the new-born King.

And angels hover in our trees
Descending from the middle sky,
On blurred, on rising falling wings,
As once on happy Bethlehem.

It is an infant, open gift
Placed by our human crib of dark:
Peace on this Eve of violence
Before the rising of the Prince.

Anxious, we watch through our black glass
The flakes fall, swirl in single file,
As sinners pondering free grace
Miss the three kings, the absent Star.

POEM FOR LENT

Is it God who thus destroys me
Feather by feather, when the wings
Subside from hover, from going over
Intense hills and meadows' drift
Green with passion, white with love?

Flight is delicious in me: to beat
Airs swarming with sun's violence;
To make steady for the single height
Where doldrum, anger, song, dove, danger
Merge—is glory, man's far-lifting gale.

But fall is sober, fall is death.
I am dropped ragged, shorn, distressed.
Little by little the ears go deaf,
The ringing goes; the bowl of fire
Tips into drab, day's routine grays.

God's hands are in this on me. He knows
That up is small steps, ten-toed, hard;
Where crowds clamor for fishes, loaves,
By some small hill on stones. Say
Nazareth or Golgotha.

EUCHARIST

Now to this Table will limp home
Unwinged, great Man, that famished bird,
From brief calamitous flight,
To taste again the marrowed Word.

O brilliant, brittle airman, he:
Riding his wonderful bones on cloud,
Warming his summer-time of flesh,
His atoms soaring and unbowed.

How bright he treads against the sun,
Icarian-sure his known, his real:
He plunges, chromosomes' Elect,
To landscapes sprouting death and steel.

So by this Board of all his doubt
He will sink down at last: wing-sweep,
Mechanic bluff, sky-swagger gone:
Un-eagled in a frightened heap.

Thus sparrowed down to zero, earth,
A smashed, sick bundle of defeat:
His beggared beak will rise, and from
Those crippled Hands take fire and eat.

A SONG FOR EASTER DAY

I saw at Easter that dread tree
On which the Christ had died.
Its blossoms were a full white fire,
Its leaves were green and wide.

And like that other tree it rose.
It had an angel stood
To guard us from immortal things
As once in Eden's wood.

It had a whirling sword for all
Afraid of holy flame
That leaps out of a burning bush
And names, O soul, thy name.

I ached before that seraph gate
And lonely looked across
As ever Adam, looking back,
Remembering his loss:

His many trees alive with fire;
His flowers, sights intense,
And every day a stinging shower
Of petalled innocence.

The striking angel is our death.
Our sins, his seven swords,
Between us and the blossoms hung
Like pentecostal words.

The tree is grace for everyman,
Love burgeons every leaf,
Sweet mercy grows on every branch,
Its dark roots nourish grief.

Christ's body still turns back the blade,
O Adam, death is gone.
We walk again the shining fields
And stand in Eden's dawn.

O STAND ME MASSIVE, THEN

O stand me massive, then,
Against all mortal evil;
Against my midnights when
My amorous devil

Shrives me as white as bone
And shrewdly winks me in
To the rituals that condone,
To the magic of more sin.

Or, when he shoulders over me,
Let heaven's tumbling dove
With bright wings hover over me
And put between us love.

From bread of stone and power,
The eucharist of mammon,
Defend me at each hour
In penitential famine.

And should I like old Faust
Against You tower me,
Or money-lend my ghost
For science on a tree:

Scatter me in anger,
Let my tongues bell wild;
Church me in the manger,
Save me in the Child.

DEATH AND RESURRECTION

I am your double man, though first you will
Me one estate: this meadowed flesh my bones
Do comfort in; the blood's warm brooks that hill
And waterfall me through; my browsing senses
Nostriled for adventure, five unicorns
That rampant in me run; the mind's huge barns
All attic'd overhead with my pretenses,
All cellared underneath with my unknowns.

And here I landlord, jubilant a while,
To store up meanings in the bins and ricks,
A sundial farmer faithful to my rites
As morning robins: except my brother, sin,
Prides in the yards and warfares at the gates.
And then my countryside is stones and sticks
And straw, and death soon wooden fences in
The ruined body of my land all still.

Yet you recover me from my disgrace.
This little ground I am, this cipher earth
I corner in, this night that densely nights
Me down to stay; you mine-field with the sun,
The fuse as long as love, the burst a birth,
A second world after the blackout's done:
And out of my debris you timber heights,
And into my despair you hammer grace.

THE WHITE TREE

It is the white blossom holds me,
The expanding air knows it,
The fair wind crushes it and me,
And we are richly rocked
In undeliberated meeting.

The tree dangles my love,
Hangs upon white magnolias
God's regular, sure, supreme speech:
Fire words, white fire, full fire,
The consumed exchange of it and me.

So a fire ring casts about us
And about the tree, undivides us,
Blows us against, between the iron gates,
By the tall angel, by his angry sword,
Penetrating me with Thee.

I know the mind's dislike of fire.
Mind is calculating, mind can count:
Beads, silver pennies, enemies.
It likes a good thing mostly.
And often, often I go
As men go in a premeditated darkness;
I make me a cringing weather,
It hems me in, churlish.

But I have seen a white tree,
Touched a voice shining.
I am undone out of my dark,
And I am found in a bright blossom.
My flight it is, my morning,
My center and my climbing.
In a white tree
I have seen Thee.

EXHIBIT

There are Debussy's skies and Van Gogh' skies
And God's skies: that is, marching skies
Full of sea air and heart's delighted distance;
Thick blue farm skies storming thick green fields,
Wide brown earth scapes, and bent men. God's skies—
What both men saw but never sang nor painted.

Debussy saw nothing, then wisp, white handful,
Swell, billow, cloud, clouds, tossing alert daylight;
He wrote the voyage from an inner island.
Van Gogh fought Christians for Christ's sake
And plotted his yellow day, marshes of violence,
And hell's bowl of heaven in Jesus' sweet name.

Both men sang and painted only one sky
And one people: God is both sailor and peasant,
Cloud and furrow, sea and farm, joy-ache.
Debussy gauged God over waves; Van Gogh by rows.
One felt thin winds, the other torrents.

Delighted God posed at every corner.

A SONG OF GRACE

God in my heart will not let go
The sheep who from His pastures run
Into the tangled lands below
Toward meadows green and flushed with sun,
Where pleasures poison to the tongue
Destroy the silly sheep with ease:
Though I the shepherd's song must sing
And call them back, because I please.

The tigers in me who maraud
My secret paths, my hidden dark,
Who prowl my blood and spring with fire
That brands me with black passion's mark;
God hunts these hunters down instead,
And feeds them more than what they lose
On Passion's Cup and Passion's Bread:
I eat, but only if I choose.

His arm has comfort for the lamb
That crippled in my forests lies,
Dangered by all the deaths I am,
In fear of all my mysteries.
He climbs the cliffs I dare not climb,
He dares the woods I dare not dare,
He saves the innocence in me:
But only if, like Him, I care.

And when from perches in the mind
My sparrows forage for the sun,
And break against the clumsy wind
And short-winged fall, collapsed, undone;
He gently with a Grace of hand
Persuades them back to placid earth,
And comforts me on human land:
But only if I know its worth.

God in my heart I know like air
Before the seasons made air sad,
But there is sadness in me where
His Love prepares me to be glad.
He is a Child whose simple song
Exclaims delight across my field,
But never a tune I hold for long,
Except I hear His joy and yield.

FALL ASTERS

The asters, pale as my weakness,
And therefore companion, reveal
Peace to the road. Walking, I hail
Them, the little blue friars,
Whose garments are meekness,
Whose scriptures start my tears.

In woods where mighty autumn turns
Blazon and maple, and air burns
With vast and clamorous events;
They tonsure blue yet stem down gray
Like a man's work or his old sin,
And so are most like mercy in

Demeanor. Such congregations pray
My need and cry as I would
Cry my adorations if I could.
Their parable is solace gnarled
With grief. Their word is penitence.
Their amen is the kneeling world.

AUTUMN SONG

It is well with the gold
Undone tongues of the fall fires
Living and dying in the leaves,
It is well with the earlier gold
When the wind's lungs blew out
The trees and gold fell like songs:
Maple goes yellow gold, oak goes
Red gold, elm goes gold gold,
And now it is well everywhere.

Words fall, and the golden children
Who have run all summer, call
Down the autumn streets, and all
Is a praise to the children:
The fires, the living and the dying,
The wind's lungs, the airs where
The leaves fall like songs: yellow
Gold, red gold, and gold gold.

And they call with a clamorous call
And listen hard. And we who have also
Run through the summer, we who are
Old, listen. It is well everywhere,
And all is a praise.

AT THE CRECHE

Stand in the stable where the birds
Of snow perform for heaven's Son
A dance of love, and one by one
Make adoration without words.

Pray by sign only, your flat hands
Open as to receive a feast
Of grace, a much for very least,
More mercy than your most demands.

Do not pray for sweet rain, nor meddle
And urge that Alice be spared her loss
Or John his pain. Later the cradle
In the true play becomes a cross.

Nor ask to be among the angels,
The high-singers in golden rings
Who praise in clamorous evangels
The friar King who out-kings kings.

Pray, rather, for a huge pity
On children, a crust of laughter
For old men, joy in our duty,
A place by the fire thereafter.

Outside the jubilant inn-cock crows
And thrice proclaims the vivid birth,
As three and thirty doves unloose
Christ's morning over Herod's earth.

THE HOLY MERRIMENT

Lo, Christ is waking, cradled in
Our loneliness, our world of night:
God-head kinged low as human sin,
Child homaged high as angeled light.

Wandering, wondering, now let all,
Through unploughed weather's burst and blow,
Harry ourselves to crib and stall,
To heaven cabined in the snow.

Let all astonished souls delight,
Have bones and ears to risk His mirth,
The holy laughter shaking night
Where God is coming into birth:

In gnarled dark death on shepherds' faces
Spacious with longing for a King,
Bold with the girth of given graces
When heaven opens and angels sing;

In Mary motionless, adrift,
Candled beside the Lamb of danger,
Perilled to mother-love the Gift,
The Cross incarnate in the manger;

In donkey, sparrows, soft-eyed ox,
Whose shuffle, whirl-wings, ancient nod,
Nuzzle and beak the Paradox:
The timeless Man in tethered God;

In Joseph darkly panicked, cheated,
Unfathered by the Fatherhood
That wills his goodness be defeated
Before the Will that wills the Good.

Declaring, adoring, all the world
Has come to be unworlded where
Levelling, loving, God has hurled
His whirlwind Truth in still, small Care

To gale down pride to stable straw,
Winnow our righteousness to chaff,
Wing-fold our grief, dove-warm and thaw
Our winter fears in Christ's bright laugh.

All's well here. The lost sons are found.
Good-will, God's Love is running sent.
All, all are savioured, all dance round
The Child in holy merriment.